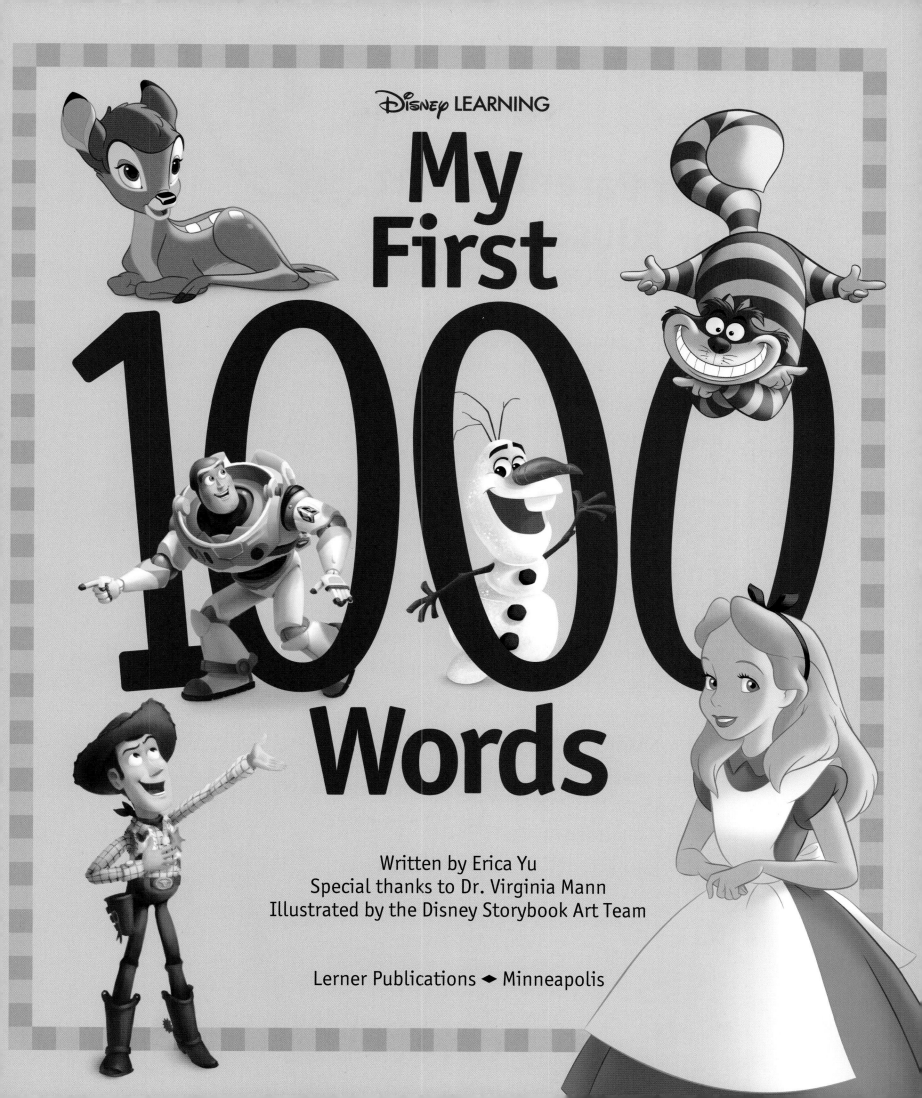

DISNEP LEARNING

My First 1000 Words

Written by Erica Yu
Special thanks to Dr. Virginia Mann
Illustrated by the Disney Storybook Art Team

Lerner Publications ◆ Minneapolis

Dear Parent or Educator,

This book is filled with beautiful illustrations of more than a thousand words, and it is designed to help young learners develop a rich, substantial vocabulary. Research shows that vocabulary is an accurate predictor of later literacy skills and school success. Finding the words to describe the world around them empowers children to express their observations, thoughts, and feelings.

Beloved Disney characters accompany your child on this journey through the wonderful world of words. The words in this book are organized into five chapters focused on different content areas. Each chapter presents a variety of engaging scenes intended to spark curiosity, imagination, and conversation. Talk about the words and pictures in this book together. Encourage your child to point out details, ask questions, and tell stories about what's on the page. Sharing this book can be a fun, meaningful family experience.

We hope this book provides an enjoyable step on your child's road to becoming a confident reader. Turn the page, and let's get started!

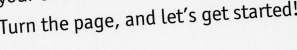

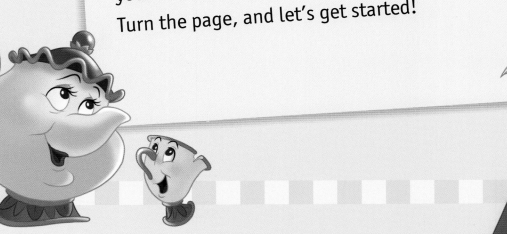

Contents

Home and

Family

Welcome! Would you like to visit Mickey's  ?

Or play in the yard with and ? Pick up a and

join for lunch. Maybe you'd enjoy some

and a . Check out Hiro's latest project

on his . And can show you what the

animals in Zootopia are wearing. Be careful not to walk in

on  in the bathroom!

All Kinds of Families!

Who's in your family? Name them!

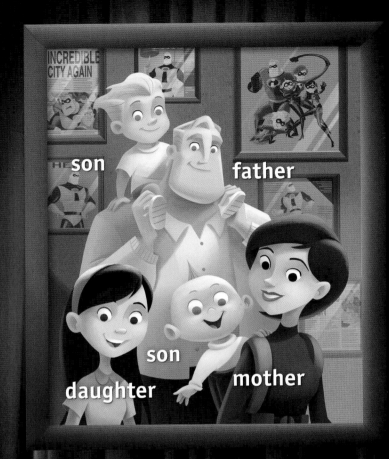

The Parr Family

Merida's Family

Mr. and Mrs. Fredricksen

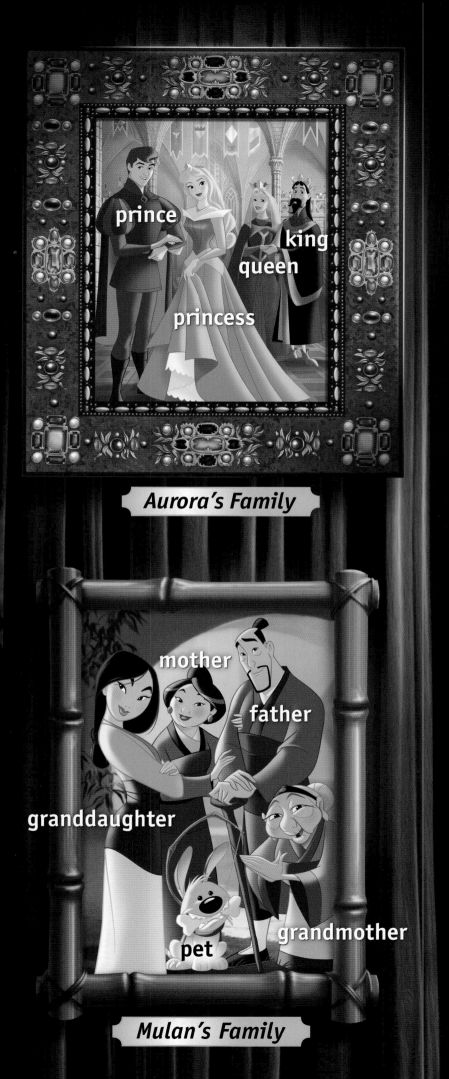

Aurora's Family

prince

princess

king

queen

Mulan's Family

mother

father

granddaughter

grandmother

pet

Donald's Family

nephew

nephew

nephew

uncle

Minnie's Family

aunt

niece

niece

Mickey's House

lawn mower

yard

porch

house

mailbox

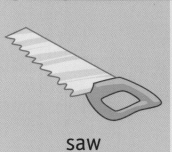

saw

toolbox

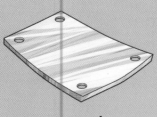

metal

wall

8

hammer

roof

letters

window

wood

door

fence

tools

driveway

Can You Find

three purple flowers?

nails

clothes

sidewalk

garage

car

9

Woody and Friends in the Yard

HOME and FAMILY

vine

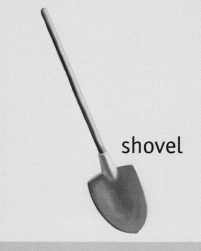

bush

shovel

stakes

Can You Find
two green aliens?

bugs

soil

water

10

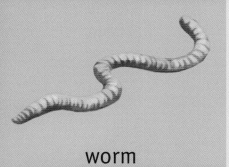

worm

bicycle

grass

hose

flowers

rake

tree

seeds

garden

snail

plants

11

The Incredibles' Living Room

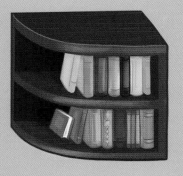

shelves

bookcase

television

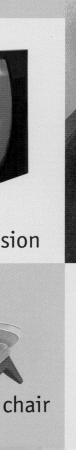

chair

vase

books

lamp

radio

clock

table

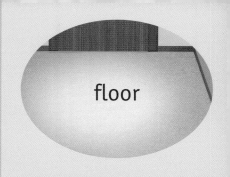

floor

vacuum cleaner

couch

photos

Can You Find five masks?

telephone

carpet

magazines

fireplace

13

Riley's Kitchen

sink

mop

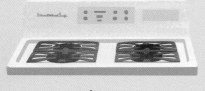

stove

garbage can

oven

iron

blender

pan

jar

sponge

kettle

pot

cabinet

garbage

refrigerator

paper towels

broom

apron

Can You Find four spoons?

toaster

can

microwave

towel

dishwasher

15

Belle and the Beast's Dining Room

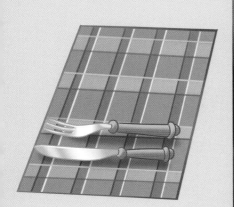

place mat

table

salt

dish

fork

cup

bowl

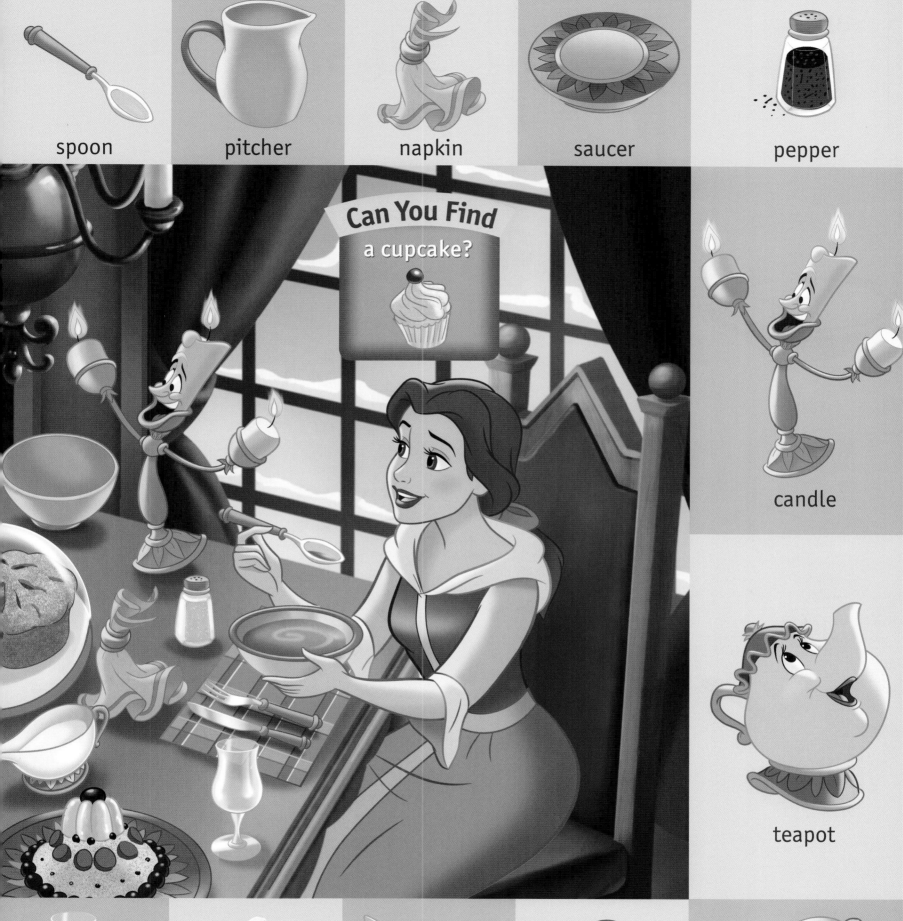

spoon

pitcher

napkin

saucer

pepper

Can You Find
a cupcake?

candle

teapot

glass

sugar

knife

butter

cream

Delicious Dishes with Remy

soup

eggs

roast beef

bacon

toast

ketchup

salad

jam

cereal

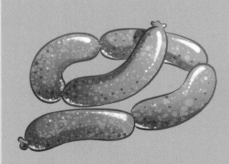

sausage

lobster

tea

steak

milk

hamburger

pasta

18

food

peanut butter

spaghetti

chicken

yogurt

french fries

sandwich

fish

bread

rice

crackers

pizza

cheese

shrimp

meat

ham

19

Food at the Market with Tiana

onion

lettuce

beet

zucchini

cauliflower

spinach

brussels sprouts

Vegetables are important ingredients in my recipes!

20

mushrooms

potatoes

beans

garlic

eggplant

vegetables

cabbage

peppers

peas

green beans

bell peppers

olives

broccoli

pumpkin

tomato

corn

carrots

pickles

celery

cucumber

21

Snow White's Fresh Fruits

pear

blackberries

melon

grapefruit

fig

raspberries

banana

papaya

coconut

blueberries

raisins

cherries

grapes

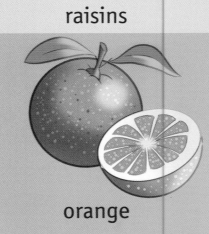

mango

orange

plum

22

peach

fruit

apple

strawberries

pineapple

avocado

lemon

watermelon

lime

I just love apples. They're wonderful in pies!

23

Hiro's Bedroom

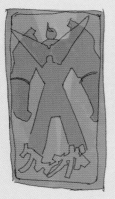

poster

closet

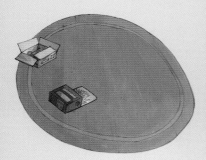

rug

socks

phone

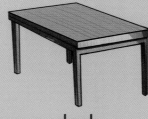

desk

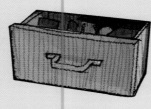

drawer

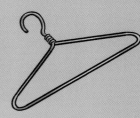

hanger

box

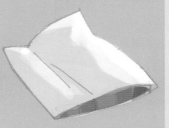
pillow

sheets

shelf

bed

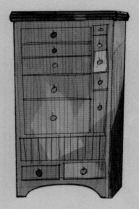
dresser

light

Can You Find
five microbots?

computer

picture

pencil

pen

shoes

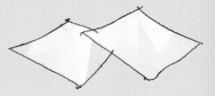
paper

25

What to Wear in Zootopia

umbrella

hat

skirt

mittens

scarf

blouse

gown

jacket

button

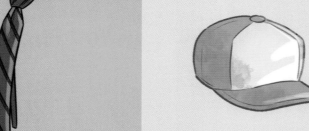
tie

cap

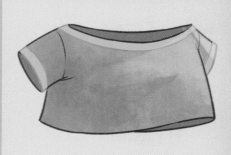
shorts

bow

coat

sweater

T-shirt

suit

cape

pants

gloves

belt

jeans

purse

raincoat

shirt

dress

In the Castle Nursery with Rapunzel

mobile

high chair

key

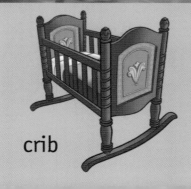

crib

bell

ring

28

crown

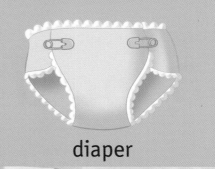

diaper

necklace

bottle

Can You Find four suns?

teddy bear

rattle

bib

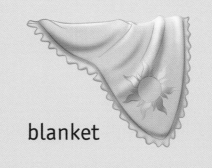

blanket

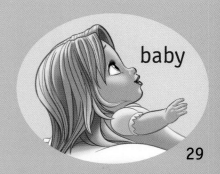

baby

29

Donald's Bathroom

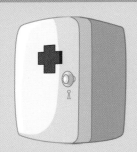

medicine cabinet

toy boat

towel bar

wallpaper

toothpaste

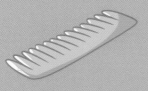

comb

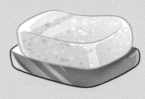

soap

washcloth

toilet paper

toothbrush

bath towel

robe

shampoo

shower

bubbles

toilet

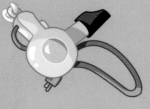
hair dryer

Can You Find

three rubber ducks?

brush

shower cap

mirror

bathtub

Town and

Community

Look at all the things to do in town! Walk around and

explore the . Dance in the village with

 and Flynn. Go to  with Mike and Sulley,

and learn something new and exciting!

Remember to bring a . You can help and

 shop for food at the market. Or visit the

for a checkup. Maybe you'd like to go for a relaxing drive

with . After your busy day, celebrate with a

at Tiana's restaurant.

Hiro and Baymax Explore the City

bus stop

office building

bus

sign

restaurant

people

stop sign

newspaper

florist

grocery store

bank

library

movie theater

buildings

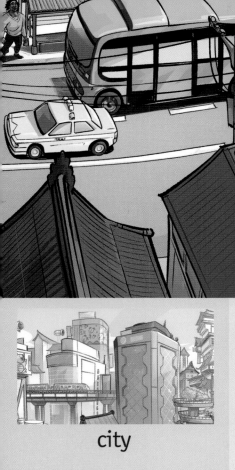

Can You Find

four lanterns?

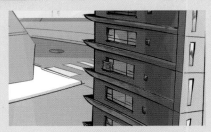

city

apartment

street

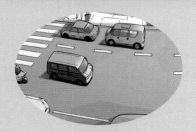

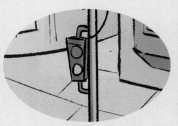

traffic light

35

TOWN and COMMUNITY

In the Village with Rapunzel and Flynn

musician

dancers

sign

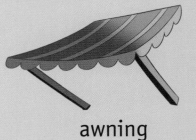

awning

bucket

flowers

36

boy

village

roof

Can You Find

two white geese?

bakery

castle

wagon

bag

chimney

girl

Mike and Sulley in School

bulletin board

notebook

chalkboard

scissors

Can You Find

six pencils?

markers

check

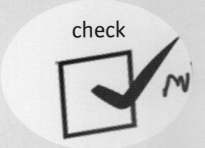

textbook

eraser

38

school

glasses

chalk

teacher

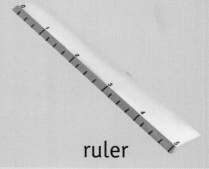
ruler

class

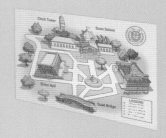
map

student

list

flag

chart

backpack

39

At Tiana's Restaurant

dessert

waiter

coins

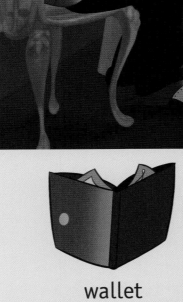

wallet

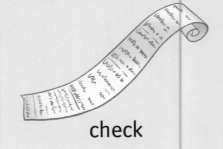

check

tray

money

ice

drinks

booth

Can You Find
four lily-shaped lights?

waitress

stairs

bottle

plate

menu

dollar bill

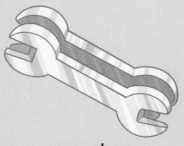

TOWN and COMMUNITY

Minnie and Friends Go Shopping

wrenches

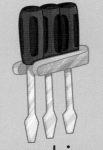

screwdrivers

silver

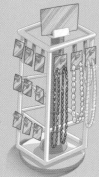

necklaces

tablet

watch

laptop computer

pliers

cell phone

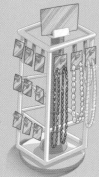

gold

headphones

beads

calculator

jewelry

MP3 player

earrings

camera

bracelets

Can You Find

two diamonds?

drill

video camera

printer

television

43

Buzz Lightyear in the Toy Store

stuffed animals

toy soldier

puzzle

doll

dinosaur

chess

video game

checkers

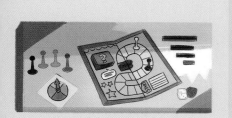

board game

action figure

yo-yo

ball

top

Can You Find

seven green army men?

blocks

toy car

toys

playing cards

piggy bank

rocket

Grocery Shopping with Lilo and Stitch

dairy

cash register

cashier

Can You Find

three pineapples?

muffins

credit card

doughnuts

flour

basket

shopping bag

syrup

seafood

shopping list

fruit punch

spices

ice cream

waffles

shopping cart

Goofy Visits the Doctor's Office

mask

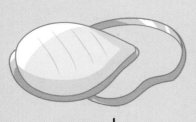
nurse

thermometer

cotton swab

scale

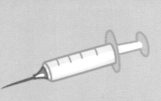
shot

file

cotton balls

doctor

needle

ice pack

bandage

X-ray

patient

cast

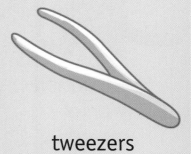

tweezers

Can You Find

two pairs of glasses?

tissues

medicine

crutches

stethoscope

Mammals at Work in Zootopia

plumber

engineer

nurse

dancer

athlete

dentist

banker

mechanic

construction worker

reporter

photographer

driver

police officer

chef

carpenter

farmers

50

clerk

singer

astronaut

doctor

secretary

firefighter

librarian

magician

painter

In Zootopia, anyone can be anything!

Lightning Goes for a Drive

pickup truck

boat

snowplow

bulldozer

ship

How about going for a drive?

Great idea!

motorcycle

van

submarine

truck

plow

ambulance

garbage truck

car

rocket ship

tractor

crane

jet

school bus

tow truck

tank

ferry

train

plane

bus

taxi

Mickey and Friends at the Airport

passenger

captain

Can You Find four stickers?

wing

sky

line

passport

airplane

luggage

propeller

helicopter

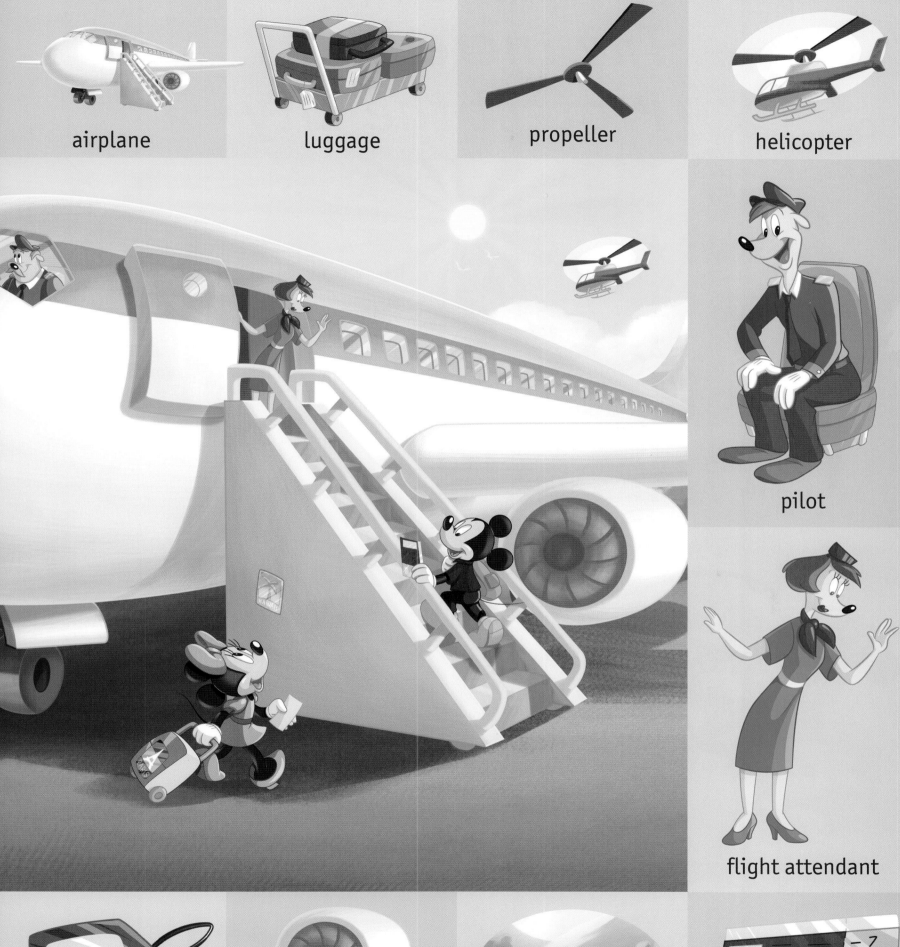

pilot

flight attendant

tag

engine

ground

ticket

The Incredibles Protect the City

postal worker

superheroes

police officer

ax

postcards

package

helmet

fire

alarm

badge

firefighter

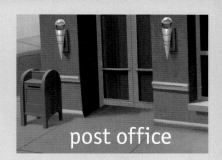
post office

POST OFFICE

Can You Find
three arrows?

ladder

heroes

stamp

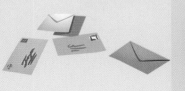
mail

fire hydrant

wheel

steel

57

Having Fun

It's a beautiful day! Let's go to the  or visit a

. Maybe you'd like to fly a  at the

park or swim at the . How about playing

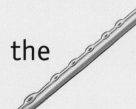? Then you could spend some quiet time

reading  and creating a . Do you play

the  or the ? There are so many fun

activities to try! What are your favorite things to do for fun?

Mickey and Minnie Plan a Day of Fun

team

fireworks

board

play

theater

roller coaster

zoo

amusement park

parade

hike

camp

Can You Find
two red pins?

circus

cage

museum

clown

61

A Picnic in Zootopia

fountain

flag

Can You Find

four doughnuts?

trash can

lake

picnic

friends

wind

bench

park

statue

kite

runner

picnic blanket

string

path

Buzz and Woody at the Playground

Can You Find five stars?

seesaw

skates

crayons

hopscotch

shovel

pail

sandbox

skateboard

handle

monkey bars

marbles

tricycle

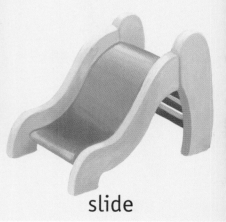

slide

play structure

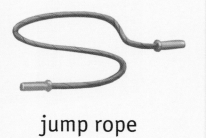

jump rope

tag

swing

bars

65

Lilo and Stitch at the Science Museum

skeleton

woman

scientist

Can You Find one clock?

robot

sun

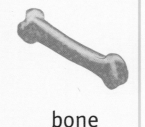

bone

stars

66

men

Earth

rock

telescope

man

children

space shuttle

moon

women

planets

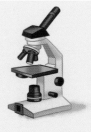
microscope

67

Making Art with Rapunzel

sculpture

paintbrush

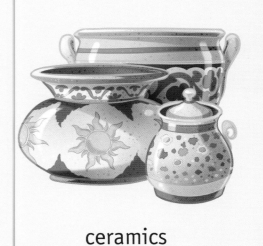

ceramics

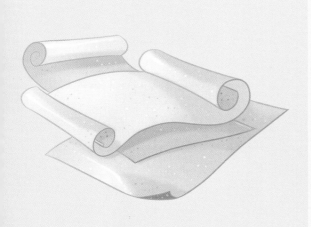

paper

sketch

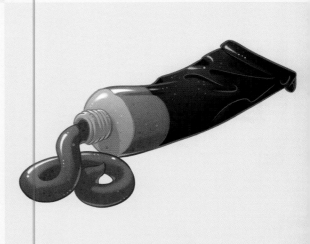

paint

artist

pottery

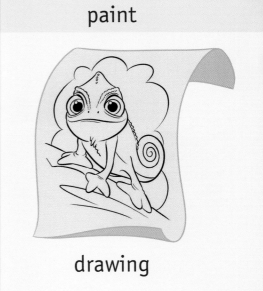

drawing

palette

clay

rag

portrait

art

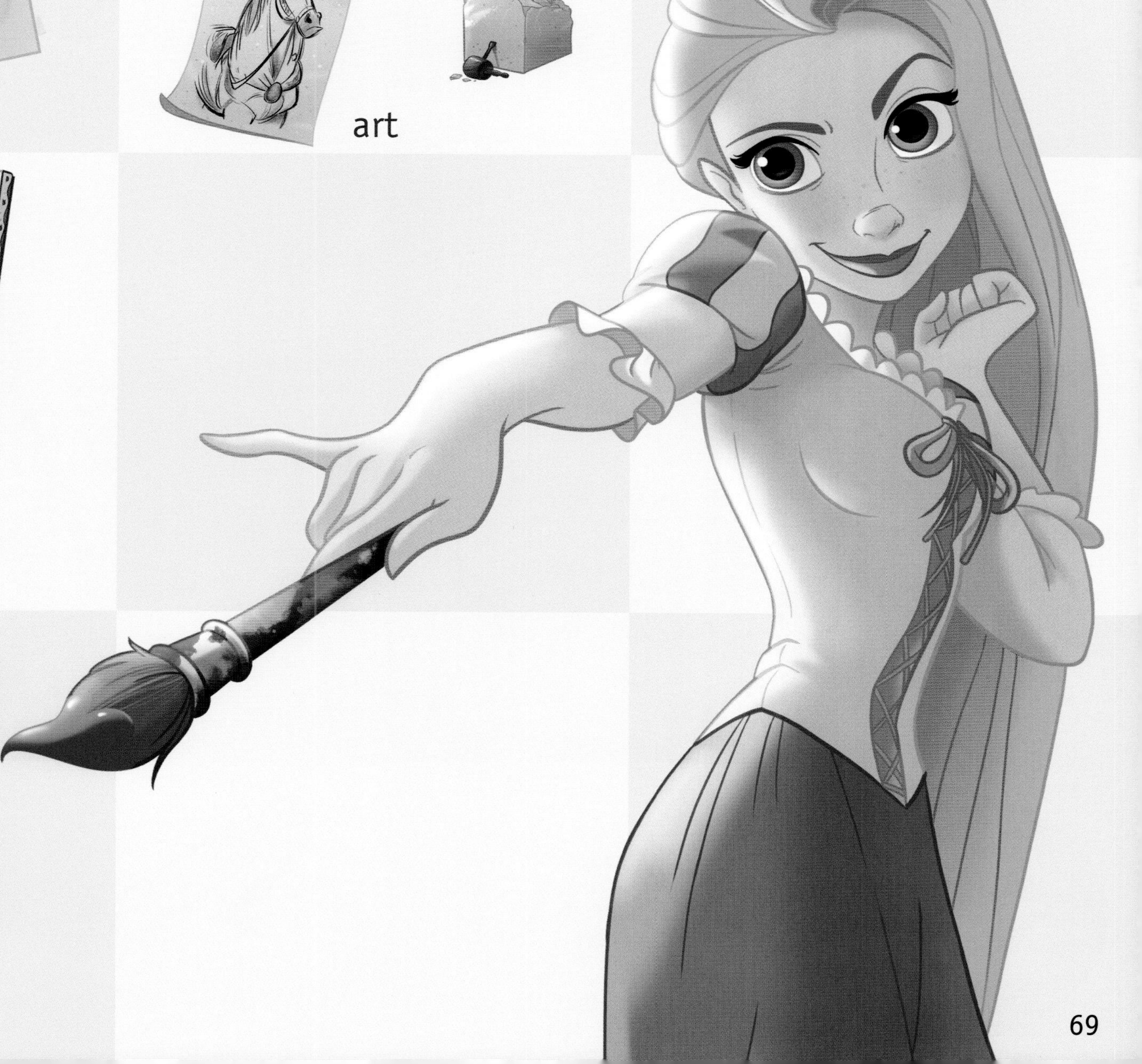

A day of making art is the best day ever!

canvas

painting

Belle and the Beast Enjoy a Day of Reading

sword

land

globe

rain

magic

bookmark

fairy

dragon

atlas

mountain

books

sails

Can You Find

Mrs. Potts and Chip?

sea

valley

ghost

storybook

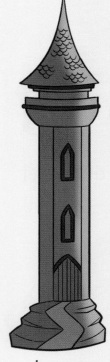
tower

71

A Concert with Ariel and Sebastian

bass

drum

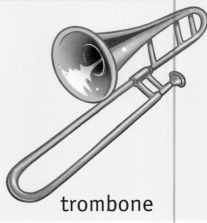

trombone

saxophone

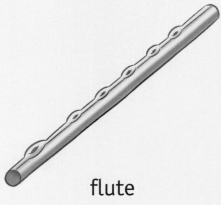

flute

tuba

xylophone

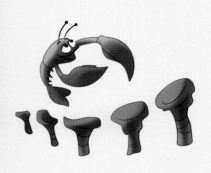

drummer

guitar

musicians

trumpet

harmonica

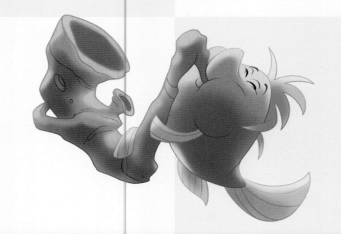

violin

harp

instruments

tambourine

band

piano

Your concerts are always amazing, Sebastian.

baton

musical notes

73

Lilo and Stitch at the Beach

sea star

ocean

sunscreen

umbrella

sand

surfboard

sun hat

shell

beach

beach ball

life jacket

beach towel

seagull

Can You Find
four shells?

lifeguard

swimsuit

wave

seaweed

sunglasses

sand castle

water bottle

Playing Sports with Mickey and Friends

skiing

soccer

baseball

basketball

There are so many sports to try! What's your favorite?

ice skating

ice hockey

tennis

football

gymnastics

cycling

archery

jogging

skating

golf

martial arts

table tennis

snowboarding

swimming

77

At the Race with Lightning

crew

fuel

Can You Find
six orange cones?

spectators

mud

springs

bolts

nuts

oil can

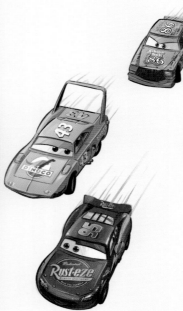

racers

tire

ramp

headphones

Monsters at the Movies

movie

curtains

projector

poster

straw

popcorn

80

 flashlight

 peanuts

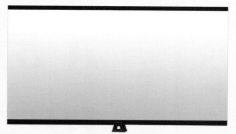 screen

Can You Find

four movie tickets?

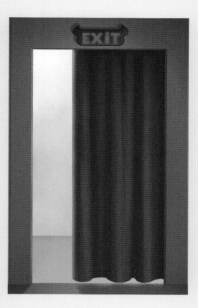 exit

 row

 seat

 soda

 actors

A Birthday Party for Anna

balloons

guests

card

candles

cookies

pie

banner

candy

cupcakes

Can You Find

three snowflakes?

cake

ribbons

presents

party hat

chocolate

juice

Belle and the Beast Celebrate Christmas

snowman

wreath

snowflakes

icicle

snowball

angel

holly

muff

ornaments

snow

sled

Can You Find

eight pinecones?

Christmas tree

tinsel

Christmas

garland

Animals

and Nature

Are you ready to meet some animal friends? Let's visit a

farm with . You can say hello to a 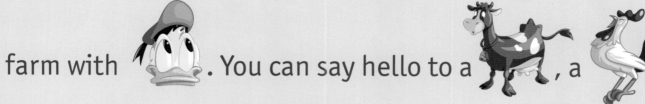, a ,

and a 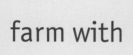. Grab some binoculars, and try to find some

animals in the wild. Look! There's a , a , and

an . Dive into the ocean with to discover

underwater creatures big and small. Take a hike in the

with Anna and Elsa. Or go camping with

and sleep under the . Nature sure is amazing!

All Kinds of Animal Friends!

What's your favorite animal?

cat

goldfish

Pinocchio's Pets

cat

cat

kittens

The Aristocats

bird

dog

dog

puppies

Lady and Tramp's Family

Bolt and His Family

cat · dog · hamster

Rapunzel's Animal Friends

lizard · horse

Pets Are Our Friends

frog · turtle · rabbit

Donald Visits a Farm

bull

hen

chicks

scarecrow

cow

rooster

donkey

lamb

90

farm

sheep

barn

turkey

horse

calf

goose

foal

Can You Find
seven eggs?

duck

goat

pig

hay

On the Plain with Simba

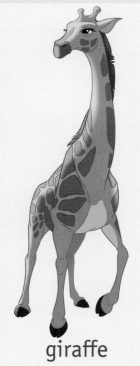

baboon

giraffe

hippo

gazelle

cheetah

leopard

92

hornbill

zebra

gorilla

hyena

Can You Find

two of Zazu's loose feathers?

lioness

lion

rhino

elephant

gnu

lion cub

93

In the Jungle with Baloo and Mowgli

bear

monkey

vulture

snakes

water buffalo

wolf

panther

crocodile

orangutan

bat

lynx

tiger

cobra

python

We're having a swinging party in the jungle!

Russell Goes Bird-Watching

woodpecker

dove

hummingbird

flamingo

crane

A Wilderness Explorer is friend to all!

parrot

bluebird

blue jay

peacock

penguin

puffin

sparrow

swan

ostrich

crow

robin

pigeon

hawk

stork

pelican

toucan

eagle

97

Bambi's Forest Friends

stag

doe

Can You Find

five acorns?

mole

chipmunk

raccoon

nest

porcupine

badger

fawn

fox

web

squirrel

moose

deer

beaver

skunk

owl

opossums

Goofy's Photo Safari

Gawrsh! Look at all these amazing animals!

apes

armadillo

chameleon

camel

coyote

jaguar

kangaroo

koala

manatee

polar bear

reindeer

panda

sloth

walrus

Nemo and Dory's Ocean World

shark

coral

kelp

clam

ray

otter

sea star

dolphin

jellyfish

sea lion

sea horse

sea turtles

ANIMALS and NATURE

102

whale

seal

octopus

clown fish

crab

squid

Just keep swimming!

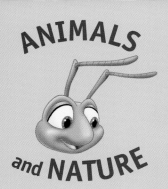

Flik and the World of Bugs

bee

firefly

ladybug

I've seen all kinds of bugs do great things!

cricket

104

ant

flea

tarantula

mosquito

hornet

moth

butterfly

dragonfly

praying mantis

spider

fly

wasp

grasshopper

caterpillar

beetle

Flowers in Wonderland

daffodil

iris

lilac

pansy

bluebells

tulip

flowers

rose

lily

lavender

carnation

violet

daisy

orchid

poppies

sunflower

You can learn a lot of things from the flowers!

An Adventure with Elsa and Anna

shadow

trail

waterfall

bark

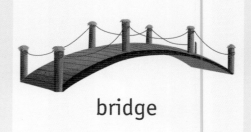

bridge

sky

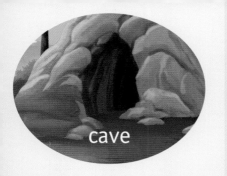
cave

rainbow

roots

hole

Can You Find

six butterflies?

branch

trees

mountain

leaf

river

cloud

sun

ANIMALS and NATURE

Peter Pan's Camping Trip

bait

forest

campfire

log

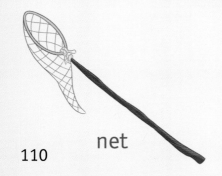
net

Can You Find

two pairs of yellow eyes hidden in the bushes?

beehive

grass

marshmallows

bushes

feather

stones

smoke

rope

moon

bats

picnic basket

sleeping bag

tent

sticks

stars

lantern

fishing rod

Things to

Know

There is so much to discover in the world around you.

Have fun counting with . Help Alice

find shapes like ●, ▲, and ■ in Wonderland.

Look at all the beautiful colors in 's shop.

Is , , or your

favorite color? Spend time with and the other

princesses to explore months and seasons. Every day is

an adventure when you're learning new things!

Parts of the Body
with Pinocchio

arm

teeth

toes

knee

tongue

neck

fingers

elbow

mouth

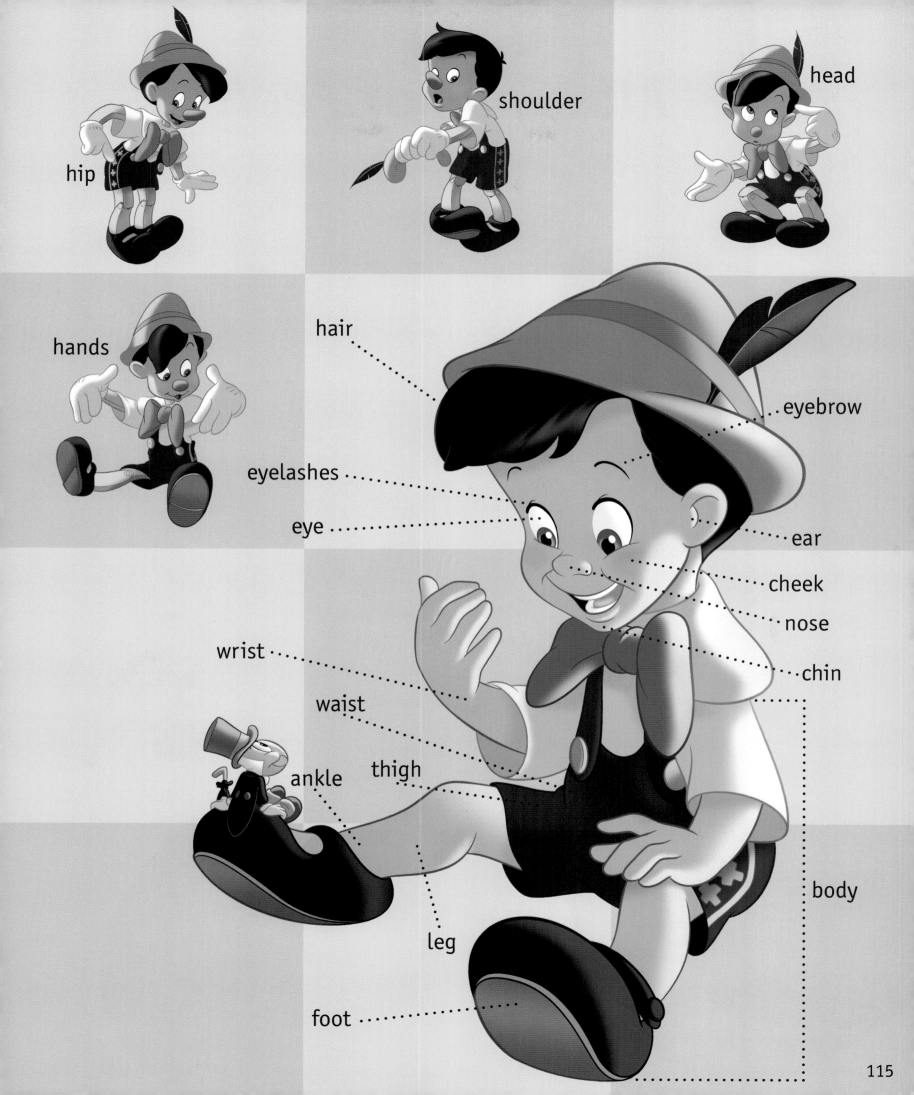

hip

shoulder

head

hands

hair

eyebrow

eyelashes

eye

ear

cheek

nose

wrist

chin

waist

thigh

ankle

body

leg

foot

All Kinds of Feelings

confident

angry

curious

nervous

proud

shy

silly

surprised

confused

scared

sleepy

sad

happy

excited

117

A Busy Year for Princesses

January

February

March

May

June

July

September

October

November

April

August

December

Seasons

spring

summer

fall

winter

Spending Time with Cinderella

morning

noon

afternoon

night

midnight

Days of the Week

Monday

Tuesday

Wednesday

Thursday

Friday

Saturday

Sunday

Counting Dalmatians

zero

one

two

three

four

five

six

seven

eight

nine

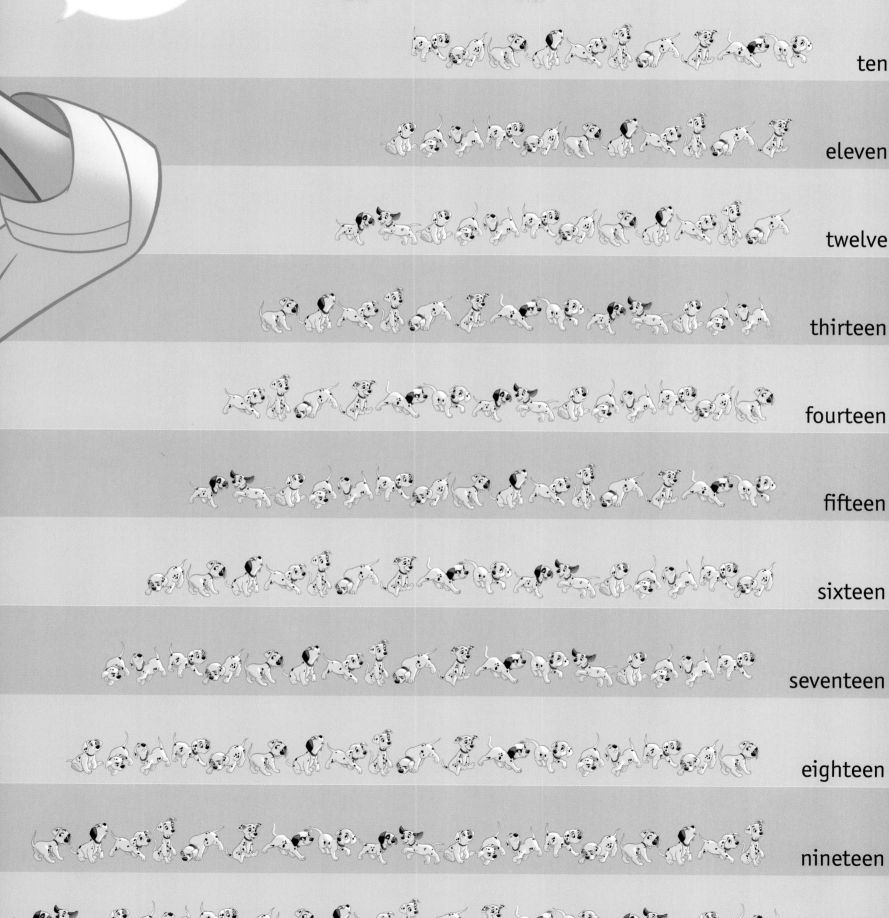

THINGS
to KNOW

Finding Shapes in Wonderland

oval

cylinder

circle

square

rectangle

heart

cone

diamond

Can You Find

four teacups?

star

crescent

cube

triangle

Cars of All Colors

red

yellow

PAINT 2 BOOTH

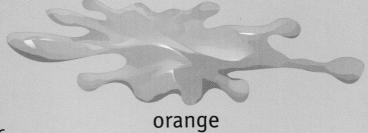

orange

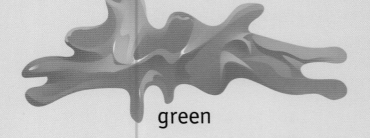

green

126

gray

white

black

brown

Can You Find?

seven paintbrushes

pink

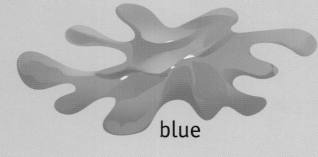

blue

purple

Olaf's Favorite Opposites

slow

fast

big

new

old

small

short

tall

closed

open

fat

thin

bad

good

dry

wet

loud

quiet

cold

hot

Busy Belle, Busy Beast

sing

talk

clean

stand

write

jump

kiss

smile

read

whisper

listen

think

laugh

dance

sleep

drink

sit

build

eat

run

wake up

131

Simba and Nala Play in the Pride Lands

near

far

left

right

above

below

through

behind

in front of

around

over

under

on

off

in

out

Olaf

Donald

Judy

Belle

Buzz Lightyear

Tiana

Daisy

Dory

Anna

Baymax

Ariel

Lilo

Mike

Simba

Nemo

Elsa

Stitch

Woody

Baloo

Rapunzel

Nick

Cinderella

Jessie

Goofy

Mulan

Sulley

Nala

Lightning
McQueen

Minnie

Lerner Publications Company
A division of Lerner Publishing Group, Inc.
241 First Avenue North
Minneapolis, MN 55401 USA

For reading levels and more information, look up this title at www.lernerbooks.com.

Main body text set in Officina Sans ITC Std.
Typeface provided by International Typeface Corp.

Library of Congress Cataloging-in-Publication Data

Names: Yu, Erica, 1975– author. | Disney Storybook Artists, illustrator.
Title: My first 1000 words / written by Erica Yu ; illustrated by the Disney
   Storybook Art Team.
Other titles: My first one thousand words
Description: Minneapolis, MN : Lerner Publications Company, A division of
   Lerner Publishing Group, Inc., [2019] | Special thanks to Dr. Virginia
   Mann. | Includes bibliographical references and index.
Identifiers: LCCN 2018033368 (print) | LCCN 2018048325 (ebook) | ISBN
   9781541543553 (eb pdf) | ISBN 9781541539129 (lb : alk. paper) | ISBN
   9781541546349 (pb : alk. paper)
Subjects: LCSH: Vocabulary—Juvenile literature. | English
   language—Glossaries, vocabularies, etc.—Juvenile literature.
Classification: LCC PE1449 (ebook) | LCC PE1449 .Y8 2019 (print) | DDC 428.1—dc23

LC record available at https://lccn.loc.gov/2018033368

Manufactured in China by Toppan Leefung Packaging and Printing (Dongguan) Co. Ltd Printed November 2019
2-48246/48245-35922/47606-8/13/2019